THE PROCRASTINATION CURE

How To Increase Productivity, And Break Bad Habits

Almost every person procrastinates at some point.

Around 90% of college students, for example, say that they engage in procrastination in general, and around 50% of them say that they procrastinate chronically. This number is lower among the general population but is still significant, since roughly 20% of adults view themselves as being chronic procrastinators, and procrastination is prevalent even among people who work in relatively prestigious professions, such as lawyers and college professors.

Understanding why procrastinators act the way that they do is important if you want to figure out how to stop being a procrastinator yourself since to figure out how to overcome your procrastination problem you must first understand the nature of your procrastination.

As such, in the following , you will learn what it means to be a procrastinator, what types of procrastinators exist, and how to tell if you are a procrastinator, before seeing what you can do to get yourself to stop procrastinating.

Procrastination is one of the main barriers blocking you from getting up, making the right decisions and even from living the dream life you painted for yourself. Recent studies have shown that people regret more the things they haven't done than the things they have done — Feelings of regret and guilt resulting from missed opportunities tend to stay with people much longer. When you procrastinate, you waste time that you could be investing in something meaningful. If you can overcome this fierce enemy, you will be able to accomplish more and in doing so better utilize the potential that life has to offer. Sometimes all our opportunities seem to be on our fingertips, but we can't seem to reach them.

Procrastination is the practice of carrying out less urgent tasks in preference to more urgent ones, or doing more pleasurable things in place of less pleasurable ones, and thus putting off impending tasks to an later time. In order for a behavior to be classified as procrastination: it must be counterproductive, needless, and delaying. Similarly, it is "to voluntarily delay an intended course of action despite expecting to be worse off for the delay."

A procrastinator is a person who delays or puts things off — like work, chores, or other actions — that should be done in a timely manner. A procrastinator is likely to leave all the Christmas shopping until December 24th.

Procrastinator comes from the Latin verb procrastinates, which means deferred until tomorrow. The prefix pro means forward, and crastinus means of or belonging to tomorrow.

Procrastination is the postponement of tasks that people want or need to do and where they know that the procrastination is probably not good and will lead to difficulties or extra stress. That is why this is sometimes referred to as an irrational delay. The term procrastination, derived from the English procrastination, is used as a professional term. When it comes to students, in addition to previous terms, it is sometimes also referred to as study-evasive behaviour.

What is a procrastinator

A procrastinator is a person who postpones decisions or actions unnecessarily. For example, a procrastinator may postpone choosing a topic for an essay that they must write, or they may postpone an assignment to complete.

Procrastinators can postpone in any area of their lives, and some people postpone in certain domains but not in others. For example, a person might be a dropout when it comes to the academic world, while someone else might be a procrastinator when it comes to their health.

In addition, procrastinators can use different methods to postpone. For example, a procrastinator can distract himself from a task by viewing social media, while another procrastinator might try to avoid having to   perform important tasks that they must complete by constantly dealing with trivial issues instead.

Common thing procrastinator do

You can procrastinate

1. Go to the doctor for an examination.

2. Call your family and friends to see how they are doing.

3. Pay your monthly bills now, so you do not have to worry about them later.

4. Update your resume and look for a job.

5. Answer your emails.

6. You always wanted to try it with this hobby.

7. Slicing junk food that we know is bad, but keep eating.

8. Get to work or school on time.

9. Do your homework now so you can relax later.

10. This man/girl is asking for a date.

11. Clean up the house.

12. Donate to the charity you always wanted.

13. Plan a vacation in a new country.

14. Finally, go to the gym and work out.

15. Have the car maintained?

16. Read the book your friend recommended to you last year.

17. Tell someone a secret that you are hiding.

18. Back to the university.

19. Apologize to someone after you hurt him.

20. Tell someone that you love him.

21. Create something artistic and share it with others.

22. Waiting for this "perfect" moment to start your own business.

23. Wash clothes.

24. Do the dishes.

25. Spend more time with your children.

26. Start with small steps towards the life of your dreams.

27. Go to a concert or sports event.

28. Learn how to speak a foreign language.

29. Take a week off work.

30. Running in a marathon.

31. I have written the book you always wanted to write.

32. Volunteer work in a local community centre.

33 Sell old things in the house that you no longer use.

34. Solve a mistake you made a long time ago.

35. Ask something because you fear the answer is no.

36. Study for an exam.

37. Go to bed at a reasonable time.

38. Have children.

39. Help a friend with something he has asked you to help him with.

40. Stop smoking.

41. Marry.

42. Shopping for food.

43. Take the garbage out.

44. Buy new clothes.

45. Get your place.

46. Saving for retirement.

47. Ending a relationship, you know does not work.

48. Try new recipes.

49. Get a haircut

50. Do something for fun.

Types of procrastination

Knowing the types of procrastination that exist is important to the extent that they do not all have the same conse□uences. Indeed, contrary to what we can think, the misperception procrastination can be very positive when is carried out an incubation of the idea during the waiting time between the goal and the action. Let's take a look at the types of procrastination.

Perfectionist procrastinator

The person is a perfectionist to the maximum for fear of being judged or ashamed. These people are so thorough with each phase that they spend too much time on the details, so they finish a lot of their projects at top speed. So, in the end, instead of avoiding mistakes, they commit them in excess, generating more fear about external judgment. In other words, they get exactly what they want to avoid, to be ashamed if something goes wrong.

Impostor procrastinator

This is one of the types of procrastination that occurs in environments with profiles that are difficult to satisfy. Therefore, the person, for fear of being described as incompetent, monopolizes an excess of work to reaffirm his responsibility, so that this attribute is associated with the image it gives. However, this attitude can lead to ac□uired helplessness, a feeling closely linked to depressive states.

Fearful procrastinator

This profile postpones his duties or obligations permanently in the face of unpleasant or boring work. This trend is closely linked to the lack of motivation inherent in jobs that become repetitive or for which the worker does not receive any type of feedback on the □uality of his work.

Submerged procrastinator

Here is another profile of procrastination. In this case, the individual has so much to do and so much in mind that he does not know where to start. It is therefore common that this leads to a mental blockage that even prevents him from starting to work. In this case of procrastination, being overwhelmed by the number of tasks can be a personal decision, or that of a person in a higher position, such as a boss, for example. Be that as it may, this excess is very negative, because it constitutes an obstacle to any progress.

Lucky procrastinator

Can we be a procrastinator and lucky? According to Neil Fiore, yes. In this case, the profile corresponds to people who consider that they work well only when they are under pressure. That is why they postpone their tasks until the last moment and find themselves at the limit to do in time what they have or intend to do.

Interestingly, individuals with this profile tend to repeat this attitude as long as they perform well. In other words, they repel their tasks until they are back to the wall. Then they take advantage of the adrenaline rush that gives them the peak of anxiety and gets to work. Of course, this way of proceeding does not work systematically.

Perfectionism and Procastination

Perfectionism is the position of a person, vis-à-vis which absolutely everything must be done in an ideal way. Perfectionism can have a pathological form, then it reveals a position in which a non-ideal result becomes unacceptable to a person. Everyone does not know what perfectionism is because the use of this term began not so long ago. Perfectionism can be a characteristic of a perfectly healthy individual or a neurotic disorder.

To understand what perfectionism is, it is necessary to consider its aspects, its signs, and its causes.

The term perfectionism means the word perfection, the desire to do everything perfectly.

Personal perfectionism manifests itself in self-censorship and invincible attraction to impeccability.

Perfectionism aimed at others is expressed by high demands, the rejection of disorder and the habit of the manifestation of the disorder.

Perfectionism vis-à-vis the world - the position of the individual, affirming the universal order, whose norms are determined by a single individual.

The socially determined perfectionism is the need to always meet the expectations of others, to respect the established norms.

What is perfectionism - the definition

There are several signs of perfectionism: scrupulousness and increased attention to minor details; the desire to bring each act to the ideal; aggressive behavior of depressive human behavior.

What is perfectionism? It is the desire to bring everything to the state of perfection that expresses itself: in the excessive concentration of the individual on the mistakes of others and personal; serious doubts about the speed and ⬚uality of the performance of its activities; excessive standards, leading to a visible decrease in satisfaction with the fruits of their activities;

- High susceptibility to high expectations;

- Strong susceptibility to criticism.

Perfectionism, as a ⬚uality, can fully satisfy a person because it teaches him to be disciplined. If it is difficult to live fully and to be mentally balanced, it is useful to determine the cause of the emergence of this ⬚uality.

The reasons for perfectionism, as well as many other mental disorders, are rooted in childhood, or rather in education. If the child was raised in an authoritarian family, then he ac⬚uires the syndrome of an excellent student, he will develop a perfectionism. Such a child proves that he deserves the attention and encouragement of his parents who are too strict.

Parents with authoritarian educational styles love to place children too high, which leads to nervous exhaustion. If children can not reach the established "norms," they are then subject to psychological abuse or physical punishment.

Perfectionism - the meaning of the word is often misinterpreted in the everyday sense. Thus, perfectionism is often confused with the strong passion of a person for any type of activity, which is not correct. A child who is a victim of domestic tyranny will naturally try to intensively remedy his shortcomings. Unlike a regular workaholic, such a child will aim to perform the necessary task, not only ⬚ualitatively but also flawlessly. This becomes the goal of the future life of the child, who will become an adult perfectionist.

A healthy perfectionism at work lies in the qualities of leadership, high efficiency, motivation, activity. In this case, the individual very soberly evaluates real abilities.

A healthy perfectionism in the work can go to the degree of mild excitement or excitement. A person who has a healthy perfectionism focuses on personal potentials and ways to reach the goal.

Perfectionism is a very controversial concept. Proponents of perfectionism, therefore, believe that a person's obsessive desire to be perfect makes him a master. Others consider perfectionism a nuisance.

Perfectionism does not allow an individual to stop, it incites him to the incessant development and learning of the new. However, the following points remain unclear: are traits of character the result of acquired perfectionism or are they conducive to the education of perfectionism?

The desire to be absolutely perfect is a laudable quality until it becomes an obsessive and persevering desire to achieve an exceptionally perfect result, correcting what will no longer require correction. Such a person devotes his personal time in vain to achieve a goal that is almost unachievable because his level of achievement is already ideal.

Thus, perfectionism forms a stable circulation, after which it turns out that a person does not do anything important for a long time. It gets something a little better, but later it all boils down to the fact that the "improvements" re□uire a major reshuffle. Therefore, the process itself becomes a boring routine that requires a lot of time and effort, which is a real disaster for personalities with a creative or professional inclination.

People with pronounced perfectionism can make a strong connection between their own sense of personal importance and performance. It turns out that a lot of time is spent paying attention to unnecessary or unimportant details, which, of course, significantly slows the pace of all work, thus reducing overall productivity.

A perfectionist tends to wait for the emergence of special conditions that will allow the ideal result of the activity to be presented immediately, completely in its final form. Such a person spends a lot of time paying too much attention to the minor details of the final product of the activity. Often, such things lose their original zest and therefore look man-made.

People with perfectionism, so as not to spoil their flawless image, are able to graciously hide their mistakes or not to embody intentions in their actions. These people consider that their position in life is all or nothing. It turns out that if perfectionists expect the ideal conditions to come true, others prefer to act in the present, even if they make mistakes.

Sometimes two concepts are used together: perfectionism and procrastination. Procrastination is a person's tendency to postpone the beginning of any work in order to do it perfectly. The problem of this behavior lies in the fact that the trial can not begin, because the more it is deferred, the more it seems depressing and unpleasant.

Perfectionism and procrastination are concepts that run out of each other, like an ardent perfectionist procrastinating to the point of feeling perfect, but that may not be the case.

Perfectionism is a ☐uality that causes problems not only to the perfectionist and the environment but also to the economic situation of a person. For example, someone who does not know how to invest in the deadlines for the mission should start from scratch or ask for an extension of time, which often leads to material costs.

It is very important to determine what are the reasons for perfectionism, which incites people to constantly seek the ideal. Many believe that all mental disorders or psychological abnormalities are generated during childhood. They are almost right, but we can not say it drastically. For example, the reasons for perfectionism can appear in adulthood.

The pace of the modern world dictates new rules, everyone wants the work to be executed perfectly. Thus, at work or in schools, institutions, people impose very high demands on them. Their realization often seems inaccessible, but a person must make efforts to "get out" of the perfect result.

Those who set the rules and the external framework do not realize how much it negatively affects the health of the individual. If you can not achieve an absolute result, although the person is willing as much as possible, she begins to doubt her knowledge and strength. The conclusion suggests that success can only be achieved by becoming the most ideal student or employee, which in fact is perfectionism.

The reasons for perfectionism come from childhood. The parental style has a direct influence on the formation of perfectionism. If parents raise their children using an authoritarian style, demanding a lot, the child is evaluated and compared all the time with the rest of the children, with classmates or friends. Little by little, the child develops the principle: when I do everything perfectly, I love myself, if I make a mistake, they will stop loving me.

Thus, many factors affect the breeding of the exaggerated demands of the child (perfectionism): evaluation constantly evolving, positive acceptance of the child only if successful, lack of stability (one day is good, the second is already bad), lack of sincere trust towards parents (child). time is worrying, it will make a mistake and disappoint them).

The second example shows that perfectionism can be formed because the parents are themselves perfectionists and therefore raise a child. They teach that everything must always be excellent and not otherwise - this is the basic rule of perfectionism.

Another type of reasons for childhood perfectionism is the style of education in which parents allow everything to the child. They make efforts so that the child can not cope with the failure so that he does not have to work too much, they flatten all the sensitive points of the child's contact with difficulties, create situations Artificial success and reward. Such "too good" parents do not realize that they are making a big mistake.

When a child grows up, he is probably confronted with the realities of life, he is not prepared for this meeting. This child feels incoherent about what he has faced and what he was before in his experience, he fails because his goals seem inaccessible. As a result, the child will believe that he can become a loser. Therefore, he will try not to fall into adverse situations but will try to do his best to become better. This overwhelming aspiration leads to the foundation of perfectionism.

If perfectionism is expressed in moderation, then all is well if it is extreme behavior, it greatly complicates the personal life of the person and affects his environment. It is quite difficult for an adult perfectionist to find friends, start a family, and not criticize those who love. He is trying to make sure everyone is following his rules and principles, which are really hard to follow.

Nobody dares to say that perfectionism is a bad and useless personality trait, the main thing in which it is "dose". If perfectionism is "normal" and is not limited to a mental disorder, it will serve as a motor to the person, stimulate the personality, contribute to success, improve the standard of living.

Pathological perfectionism, on the contrary, hinders the development of the personality, contributes to the destruction of the personality itself, of all that surrounds it and of the quality of life in general. The owners of the "syndrome of excellence" (perfectionism) are obliged to know to what extent they can use their character traits and orient them correctly.

The pathological form of perfectionism has such an impact, in which a person's life position changes, he declares that others are obliged to respect them. Thus, the perfectionist consciousness encourages a person to put everything under his frame and to embrace the rest.

One can perfectly remind a perfectionist that he has problems as to the perception of the world and himself, stating that he establishes high and exorbitant surveys and objectives that he proposes to achieve, goals that is is often unrealistic to realize. But one can only waste time because the reaction of the perfectionist to all his statements will be the denial, the protection of his own positions and the rejection of the opinion of another person.

If, over time, the perfectionist himself realized that he felt the complexity of his being, using such attitudes, or that life itself adapts and that he is obliged to look at oneself, to understand that life positions are not constructive, so only maybe someone will want to change. It is impossible to eradicate perfectionist installations to the end, but it is quite possible to concentrate them constructively and to modify them a little.

There are at least seven operations involved in this process of perfectionist procrastination. (1) You adhere to high standards. (2) You have no guarantee that you will do well enough. (3) Less than the best is not an option. (4) If you think things are not going well enough, you feel uncomfortable. (5) You are afraid of feelings of discomfort. (6) You hide your imperfections and avoid discomfort by doing something "safer", like playing computer games. (7) You repeat this annoying process until you get away from this contingent ride by working to do better without seeking perfection from yourself.

Break a Perfectionism-Procrastination Connection

When perfectionism and procrastination combine, you can become your own worst enemy. By freeing yourself from this complex process, you can use your time better to achieve more with less stress. Here you see an example of how this process works, an example of a case and some ideas to break the link between perfectionism and procrastination.

If you are concerned about poor performance and anxiety, what you fear is based on what you think of yourself if you fail or how others may judge you. Consider your achievements as success or failure. failures and measures of your personal value. This thought of conditional fear of value is a form of dichotomous thinking. According to this assessment process, you are a winner or a loser, worthy or worthless, strong or weak. For example, you expect and require at least one B + class. The goal is reasonable. The wait is not like that. You get a B and you feel like a failure.

In a perfectionist world with strong beliefs, it is not enough to do well enough; you have to do it very well. It is not enough to have typical designs. they must be exceptional. When achieving perfection becomes a contingency of value, it is understandable that fear is a common conse□uence.

Perfectionism is a risk factor for fear of failure and procrastination. You expect great performance. You doubt whether you can achieve perfection. You want to alternate and do something less threatening. You wait until you can be perfect. This is an example of procrastination aimed at perfectionism.

How to get rid of perfectionism

How to manage perfectionism? It's a question that takes less the perfectionist than those around him. To whom it is common to communicate with a perfectionist, they complain about his demanding behavior.

To overcome perfectionism, a person must adhere to certain techni ues. Before starting to perform a specific task, you must first formulate the objective itself, then the criteria for determining the qualitative performance of the task. Then, you must create an installation for the "Out of Task" inadmissibility. Then, it turns out that thanks to the criteria and the installation, the person will be able to understand that he has finished the task and that the "final result" will not be necessary for anyone.

A number of success criteria must include the price of the achievement. Often, because of the persecution for quality, perfectionists forget the price. Therefore, it is necessary to clearly define the limits of an acceptable price for the result. This prize must consist not only of money but also of the forces expanded, health and negative experiences.

The list of criteria should also include the time spent to achieve the goal. Not only will the task be well completed, but it will have to be completed in time. Therefore, it is extremely important to establish a time period beyond which it is necessary to stop increasing the uality of the performance.

If a person is concerned about their behavior, if they want to change themselves and become interested in the treatment of perfectionism, the bottom line is to understand that it is impossible for everyone to love and work so that everything the world can please. If you like the result of the job and the person did it, you do not have to do it too much. Anyway, there are people who do not like the result. In fact, therefore, it is not necessary to correct a hundred times your report, plan, presentation or another professional result. Maybe not everyone will be pleased with the work presented, but one hundred percent will find those who will love everything, or even find it perfect.

Developing the ability to delegate business will help a person get rid of perfectionism. It is very difficult to entrust the work to a perfectionist person because she is nervous and doubts the quality of the performance. This often occurs in group work, where workers or students are divided into subgroups, to which they are assigned a task and to the implementation, to which each must contribute. The perfectionist does not trust the abilities of other personalities and takes responsibility for all that is accomplished.

That's why a perfectionist should start learning to transfer some of the responsibilities to others. It should not be directly related to work alone. You can start with housework: ironing, cooking, cleaning. The essential thing is to entrust the work to other people and not to observe the process, not to do it again later, in our own way. Little by little, people get used to it.

Leave the job well done, but do not dwell on looking for defects. A person who wants to reduce the manifestations of obsessive perfectionism should not forget to draw up a list of future business for tomorrow. Once the compilation is complete, carefully review important tasks and record only the most important and urgent tasks. So you do not have to keep everything in your head, the tasks will be completed more quickly because by looking at the list, the individual will see that there is no time to modify or correct something because you have to do more things.

How to manage perfectionism?

This will help to list the losses resulting from the increased demands placed on life, on others and on themselves. A person should think about the number of wonderful moments of his life he missed, the number of parents he lost, and the nerves he spent.

You must analyze your fears of not being executed. If a person is afraid of not having the time to do it perfectly, it means that you have to start doing it and not to procrastinate it, and if the time has come, you have to show the result, what it is that time. Any mistake must be made in the path of success. Once the errors of the experiment have been learned, it is possible to predict the probable repetition of an error.

You have to learn to identify and share the main and the least important. This speed is the □uality criterion. Therefore, in the work process, it is not necessary to dwell on minute details and on their treatment, it is necessary to highlight the main aspects and work on them.

If there is a possibility, you should take a break to evaluate the result of the job with a new look. There is a high probability that it will not be as serious as it seemed at once. Once a week, there must be a compulsory rest. At rest, it is necessary to forget the work, the future, and past affairs, to do nothing.

When considering your to-do list, it's important to choose a task that can not be accomplished one hundred percent, but that allows for imperfection, but not in a serious way. For example, instead of a jacket, wear a cardigan, paint your hair differently, change the habits of individual nutrition, adjust the mode of the day. Gradually, it will be understood that without perfectionism, it is much more interesting and easier to live.

About stress, anxiety, and procrastination

All living things are under pressure. A pigeon can feel stressed when predators are close or when the temperature changes quickly or when food is scarce. A new job is stressful until you adapt. You have a schedule that you must follow and you are stuck in traffic. It can be stressful.

Your stress level influences what you do. When you are distracted by stress, you run the risk of delaying your activities and experiencing procrastination. This is where you feel stressed, postponed and feel stressed by thinking about what you have not done. By doing this, you leave more unresolved things and you feel overwhelmed. It is a classic vicious circle.

When your body and mind are calm, you will probably feel the control. You see opportunities to build a better future. By taking advantage of these opportunities, you increase your confidence faster by taking on the challenges. You have less time for procrastination and you risk less procrastination. You can always feel stressed by the change, but you will bounce faster.

You can reduce stress by soothing your mind and body. Meditation, for example, is a way to do this based on evidence. Put yourself in a comfortable and □uiet place where you are safe from interruptions. Five minutes in the morning and five minutes in the afternoon humming a single word, such as "One." During a period of six weeks, you can feel calmer.

By increasing your feelings of peace, you build up emotional reserves. With deeper emotional reserves, you are less likely to fall into a pattern of secondary procrastination. This is where the stress (anxiety, depressed mood, etc.) precedes the delay and the consequences of this delay lead to more stress. You can use these reserves with confidence to overcome recurring fears.

About fear

Fear is a fear of something that can happen □uickly or in the distant future. You are vigilant. You are on your guard. This sense of integrated survival is strong enough to prevent you from experiencing real threats.

Parasitic fear is different. When you are anxious about fear, you exaggerate the risks and dangers or you create non-existent risks.

Your parasitic fears concern you normally. For instance

You expect that you will not be effective and that you will feel exhausted.

You feel anxious and think that you cannot control these feelings.

You insist that you ridicule yourself in public and believe that you cannot prevent this result.

You panic because you lose control and do not bounce.

You are afraid that you will not pass a test and think that you cannot change this result.

Each of the examples above suggests impotent thinking accompanied by feelings of parasitic anxiety. Can you try it in a different way?

Change anxious thoughts, feelings, and actions

Your parasitic fears start with a prediction of an exaggerated danger or based on a fiction. A solution is to eliminate friction. Let us see an example of concern about the possibility of public ridicule.

WHO SAYS PROCRASTINATION SAYS STRESS!

After procrastinating too much, it's the stress that takes over. Not being able to complete the tasks within the predefined timeframe generates stress. However, its hold over too long can have devastating conse☐uences in our lives.

Excess stress is, therefore, a problem that affects the majority of workers. In addition to the loss of considerable time and energy - nothing is more tiring than a job that you continually push back.

Fighting procrastination involves an understanding of the cause. Several factors are at the origin of this phenomenon:

The combination of obligations and tasks can make some people anxious or they do not feel an interest in doing them. It may seem impossible to fill everything.

The social pressure can also be the cause. Some people want so much to improve themselves and do not feel any desire to fulfill the missions which are entrusted to them if these do not reflect the perfection so much expected. As a result, they spend too much time fine-tuning every detail and thus delay to complete their work. Behind a procrastinator hides a perfectionist!

The fear of failure generates, in this step, stress that blocks many people (especially if they set themselves unachievable goals). This fear leads to finding - consciously or otherwise - a whole other distraction to spend their time and thus avoid being confronted with what scares them.

Discover how to beat stress and procrastination.

ORGANIZE YOURSELF!

You surf too much on the internet, talk to your colleagues while you have some work to do? When you procrastinate, your productivity is directly felt! On the day you are late, stressed, and have trouble managing your time.

You will be the one who will progress very slowly in the hierarchy of the company in addition to botching at the last minute of your work. Use your best efforts to organize your time, as well as the crucial tasks you most likely postpone to the next day.

SPLIT YOUR TASKS!

Adopt the method! This consists of cutting an activity into slices, to make it more edible. Identify a beginning and an end. If you have, for example, a report to do, create a file first, make a summary, checkpoints, read again ...

In addition, set your own deadline when your goal should be reached. Tip: Overestimate the amount of time you will spend doing a task. (Multiply by 2 or even 3). In this way, you will be better able to manage the imponderables and avoid disappointments.

DARE FIVE-MINUTE PLANS!

You have to accumulate emails and other tasks to complete, try to deal with the case for only five minutes. It's up to you to see if you want to follow another plan.

So you contain your frustration and do something unpleasant not too long. Thus, self-esteem reaches, from this step, its culminating point for having accomplished a daunting task or deemed difficult. The pleasure is even at the rendezvous!

TRUST THE DIGITAL!

Tools exist to help you manage your tendency to procrastinate. The plugin LeechBlock for Firefox allows limiting the duration of connection to certain sites. For example, if you spend far too much time on Facebook, you can limit your access to 15 minutes a day for example, or 5 minutes every 3 hours.

This tool will permanently change your habits. In addition, RescueTime software is also very interesting for you to realize the time lost. This software logs everything you do, and you'll be able to see the reports and see at the end of the week what percentage of your time on the computer has been productive and how much time has been spent on unnecessary activities.

IDENTIFY WHAT YOU HAVE TO LOSE!

Choosing is so difficult that often you can feel paralyzed at the thought of moving. If you feel overwhelmed, you should go back to very simple things like listing the pros and cons of procrastinating in a particular situation.

When you call on your conscience for your actions or inactions and sort out the benefits, you release your mind. This makes it possible to see more clearly what emerges from it and to visualize the conse□uences of our inaction.

TAKE ADVANTAGE OF THE STRESS!

Stress, in small doses, can help you be more productive by providing a little boost of adrenaline that allows us to be effective, alert and □uick-witted. This "good stress" is short-lived if you do not let it overwhelm you. To avoid being overwhelmed, make a checklist and tick boxes to not forget anything.

Take a blank piece of paper, list all the tasks to be done during the day and during the week. Ticking the boxes provides a real sense of satisfaction and motivation to follow the schedule.

PUT SOME MUSIC!

Classical music has a real soothing effect on your whole being. It slows the heart rate, lowers blood pressure and even decreases stress hormone levels. The music you love fills your brain with neurohormones of well-being, including dopamine.

In addition, it soothes anxiety and stress on a daily basis. Some research has shown that it is particularly beneficial for people who experience stressful events, such as surgery. If you do not have headphones at hand, try humming or playing your own music. After all, music softens manners!

STAY ZEN!

Procrastination can generate a feeling of stress, accentuating your sense of dispersion. To refocus in the present moment and be able to take action, breathing exercises can be practiced for three minutes. These exercises reduce tension and relieve stress by supplementing with oxygen. Indeed, every yogi thinks that breathing - known as pranayama or "life force" - nourishes the body.

CONGRATULATE YOURSELF

Before you tackle your to-do list, set a reward to motivate yourself. Be happy with yourself when you have completed a pesky task. Even if it's a five-minute plan. Give yourself a coffee, an outing with a friend or even a relaxing time in the sun and you will leave again.

LAZINESS AND PROCRASTINATION

Laziness is a difficult discipline

No, that's not right. But the truth is: general activity is in vogue today. Where do you still see today people who just sit around or sit around, watching people pass by and their thoughts while transfiguring? Instead, the smartphone is pulled out immediately, checked e-mails and then shot a selfie. The timeline could look suspiciously inactive.

Today, we are crazy about work. We fight laziness and try to defeat them where we can. And it's due to industrialization and morality. With the Reformation and increasing productivity, employment became a virtue and a lazy person became a sinful dishonor. Even Martin Luther scolded: "No one dies from work, but from idleness and idleness people come for body and life; because the man was born to work as the bird to fly. "And when he was chancellor Gerhard Schroeder railed:" There is no right to laziness. "One could also say: the sweet idleness - it is now highly suspicious, almost it even looks parasitic.

No desire? So you get laziness and discomfort under control

Laziness does not have a good reputation, but on the other hand, it can be so relaxing, just not doing anything. Especially in times of great stress, there is absolutely nothing wrong with it when everyone takes the time to indulge in a bit of laziness. What could be better than spending a Sunday in the hammock in the garden, listening to the birdsong and fading out the problems for a few hours?

From soothing laziness, however, persistent demotivation and aversion develop, which becomes a chronic permanent state. If one has done something good with the well-deserved time-out from the work-addiction, the unpleasure becomes a problem.

Even simple tasks become increasingly difficult, the procrastination becomes the main occupation and unfortunately, the lack of drive also shows in the job.

Call it laziness, laziness, indolence or anything you want, but the idea of doing nothing when things have to be done is often seen as a sign of weakness and flight. You may be lazy when you do not want to deal with something, such as a boring chore or a difficult confrontation with someone. You might be lazy because you feel overwhelmed and think the task should be done by an entire team and not just you. And then there are all those times where you just do not feel like it. In any case, most are not a desirable trait.

But even acute unpleasure can be outsmarted. We have some tips on how to find new energy and motivation:

Make a change

Sometimes we need a change of scenery to rekindle the lost motivation. The same rooms, the same faces, the same impressions. The unchanging environment can lead to displeasure, but when you surround yourself with fresh impressions and other - preferably highly motivated colleagues - the energy is on and you overcome his lethargy.

Make your goals public

A particularly easy way to get your own laziness under control: Tell as many people as possible of your goals and intentions. These can be friends, family or colleagues. You want to learn a new language, do more sports or do training to finally make the next career move? The more people know about it, the more binding this goal becomes for you. To benefit from this effect as long as possible, you should always keep the initiates up to date. What have you already done and what's next? The praise for their own efforts acts as an additional impulse against laziness.

Look for fellow combatants

If you do not want to tackle something on your own, a competitor can bring back the necessary motivation. One can perhaps satisfy oneself with threadbare excuses and justify one's idleness, but if a partner comes into play, one is more likely to jump over his shadow.

Keep track of your progress

Being aware of how much you have achieved with your work can be very motivating. You can do this, for example, in the form of a ToDo list, where you check off or cross out all the tasks that are done. Or you can always make a small motivational note when you reach your daily goal.

Rethink your way of working

With time, a certain routine creeps into everyday life for everyone. And in the end, the air is out. Being aware of and questioning such habits can be an important step in increasing your motivation. Sometimes it is enough to devote yourself first to the unpleasant tasks.

Recognize the value of your time

Have you ever thought about how much time you spend doing nothing because you do not feel like it? After you have dealt with this thought, the next question inevitably follows: What could you do with your free time if your initial laziness did not stand in your way? Perhaps you would be much earlier finished with a project that would have less stress, could an earlier closing time to enjoy, time for a hobby finds. Your own time is a valuable asset that you should treat in the same way.

Use the 2-minute rule

A simple motto to tackle things and fight the idleness and the reluctance: If you can do something in 2 minutes or less, do it now. This puts an end to unnecessary postponing of small tasks and motivates you by noticing that you are actually doing something.

Determine the real problem. Whenever the lazy monster threatens to take over your motivation, take a step back and try to assess what's really going on. Laziness is usually a symptom and not a problem in itself. What is the cause of your lack of motivation? Are you tired, overwhelmed, scared, hurt or just uninspired and stuck? The problem is usually smaller than you think and you can overcome it quite easily.

Whatever the problem that prevents you from moving forward, do your best to solve it. In most cases, it will be just a detail or a specific problem. Finding the cause is the only way to solve your problem.

Concentrate on the problem itself. Now that you think you've found the cause of your laziness, focus on it. It may not be an easy solution, but it will be final. Consider the following points.

If you are tired, start taking the time to relax. Everyone needs time to relax. If your schedule does not allow it, you will have to make sacrifices. But the benefits you derive from it will only be better.

If you are overwhelmed by the events, take a step back. How can you simplify what you have to do? Can you divide it into several small tasks? Can you make a list of priorities and manage each priority one after the other?

If you are scared, what are you afraid of? Obviously, there is something you would like to do. Are you afraid of succeeding?

To finally reach your goals and be unhappy? How can you understand that your fear is not rational?

If you are hurt, the only answer may be the weather. The pain, sorrow and all these negative emotions will not dissipate on demand. Your injuries will need time to heal. Putting less pressure on your shoulders to get back on top could be the trigger for the change you want.

If you lack inspiration, what can you change in your habits? Can you expose yourself to a new environment or is there a mind demon you will need to conquer? How can you improve each day? Think of it in terms of meaning: music, food, sight, sounds, etc.

Get organized. Being surrounded by bazaar, even if it is only visual, can be an important brake on our motivation. Do everything you can to organize yourself as well as possible. Whether it's your office, your car, your house, your life, tidy up.

Our subconscious has an impact on our lives that we often do not take into account. Whether it is unpleasant colors, poor lighting or lack of balance in our environment, it impacts our mind. Get rid of these subtle but powerful deterrents by organizing yourself at best.

Watch your speech. Behaviors sometimes lead to thoughts and other times thoughts cause behaviors. Cover your backs and get rid of your negative internal dialogue. Thinking "I'm so lazy, I'm not good for anything", will not get you anywhere. Stop right now. You only have control over the speech that you are repeating yourself.

Whenever you find yourself not doing your best, turn it positive: "I've been slow this morning, but now is the time to start. I will finish all this this afternoon! You will be surprised to see that this momentum of positivity could really change your mindset.

Be careful. So many of us do not take the time to stop to smell the scent of roses. We ship a good meal only to get dessert, wine or bed faster with a full stomach. We always think about what we will do next instead of living in the present moment, which is wonderful though. By starting to live in the present, you will learn to enjoy it.

The next time you find yourself thinking about the past or the future, come back to the present. Whether it's the landscape around you, the food on your plate or the music you hear, let the present show you how good it is to be on Earth and live. Sometimes slowing the train of life or stopping it completely can give us the energy to make the most of what we have.

Think of the benefits. Well, you are now focused on the present. Let's focus now on a better present. What would happen if you enjoyed the moment? What would happen if instead of losing your morning lying in bed you get up and do yoga, finish your work and make a good breakfast? What would happen if you did this almost every day for the next 6 months?

It would be wonderful, that's it! Let these positive ideas take control of your thoughts. And realize that once you start and develop this habit, everything else will come easier.

Start. There is a beginning to everything, even if it is only a matter of removing the staples from the papers you need to file or scrape off your windshield to get onto the highway. Overcoming the initial inertia naturally felt by most of us in difficult situations or tasks will put you on the right track. You will also see step by step how to move towards your goal. Eating your bite-sized elephant will help you gain momentum and you'll gain enough self-confidence to stay motivated and find things less daunting.

To expect from life that it is easy is not realistic, life is often difficult and sometimes even very difficult. But life is wonderful, surprising, exciting and full of hope. By being lazy, you exclude yourself from the possibilities that life offers you, which is self-destructive behavior. By improving your attitude to the hazards of life and learning to tolerate the things that affect you, you will develop your resolve and become more constructive. As soon as something seems insurmountable, difficult and undesirable, immediately attack this task. Do not think twice, do not find an excuse, do not avoid it: immerse yourself in this task.

The five-second method can work for you. When you're stressed or want to daydream, give yourself five seconds to resume your activity. This allows you to avoid going around in circles and keeps you busy.

Take your time. It is important to divide the work into several stages. The smaller the steps, the more accessible they will be and the more feasible they will be. By actively seeking a way to accomplish a task or achieving a goal that requires you to exercise control and mastery of yourself, you will feel empowered and not threatened. In many cases, laziness arises from feeling overwhelmed by events. You give up then even before having started, because the mental disorder you are facing seems too important to you. The secret is then to trust the power of little things.

This does not mean that you can not alternate tasks, you can and diversity is essential to maintain your interest. This means that you will have to do each little task separately, separating them in a clear way, instead of poking right and left at the same time. As you move from one task to another, stop at a breakpoint, so that you can easily get back to work when you return to this task.

It is often said that people who complain about not having enough time lose it stupidly, like doing many things at once. When forced to do many things in a short time, the human brain does not work effectively. In other words, multitasking undermines our intellectual abilities. Free yourself by doing what you have to do in order, without guilt.

Learn to motivate yourself by the speech. You will be your own coach, your own source of inspiration. Take action by telling yourself motivating things and affirming your actions. Repeat for example "I want to do it and I do it now! And "I'll take a break when I'm done, and this break will be well deserved." If necessary, tell yourself these things out loud. By giving voice to your actions, you will feel motivated.

Reciting a rewarding mantra throughout the day could help you stay motivated. Repeat for example "I can do it, I can do it". You can also visualize certain activities as if they were accomplished and thus anticipate the feeling of success you will feel.

Learn to reward yourself for the very little things you do or try to achieve. The rewards will soften the tasks and help you continue your efforts. If you manage to do something that you can not do the day before or that you dread a lot, you deserve a great reward. By rewarding you with each little success of the path, you reinforce in you the idea that you are on the right track. Choose simple but effective rewards, such as an extended break, a movie, indulging yourself with a good dessert (from time to time) or similar things. Leave the big rewards for the end goal. By using this reward system, you will train your mind to actively seek to work for this reward.

Breaks are both a reward and a necessity. Do not confuse the need to regularly take short breaks to breathe and nurture your creativity with laziness.

Obviously, the opposite of reward is punishment. People respond better to positive stimulations and it is better to stick to rewards. Punishing you for not achieving your goals will turn against you, confirming your beliefs that you are lazy and worthless. It is absolutely useless.

Procrastination at work: the causes

Let's first say that procrastination is not a new phenomenon. This word was introduced in the French language in the 16th century, probably imported from Italy. But in Greek antiquity, it was already well known. Thus the philosopher Democritus wrote: "Always post things and you will never reach your goals." But, the scale of the phenomenon today is explained by the fact that our time is singular. To understand the mechanics leading to procrastination, we will do a simple exercise: Close your eyes and think about your work ... What word comes to your mind? What word do you associate with this work? For the majority of you, the term appeared to have a more negative than positive connotation. Today, few employees associate the word "pleasure" with their job. In 2010, a study in Canada, "General Social Survey," found that 27% of Canadians rated their workdays as "extremely" or "somewhat" stressful. Of these, 62% said work was their main cause of stress. But, let's look at France. The newspaper Le Monde of 19 May 2013 described France as "champion of stress at work". Based on a study commissioned by the European Commission, "Third European Quality of the live survey", the daily showed that the Hexagon is handicapped by a particularly high rate of work stress. The newspaper Le Monde of 19 May 2013 described France as "champion of stress at work". Based on a study commissioned by the European Commission, "Third European Quality of the live survey", the daily showed that the Hexagon is handicapped by a particularly high rate of work stress. The newspaper Le Monde of 19 May 2013 described France as "champion of stress at work". Based on a study commissioned by the European Commission, "Third European Quality of the live survey", the daily showed that the Hexagon is handicapped by a particularly high rate of work stress.

So, as we understand it, the first lever of procrastination at work touches on the vision that many employees have of their activity. They do not associate it with pleasure. It is an obligation, necessity, the only way to make a living. Even if it is unsaid, work is in the minds of some employees a form of enslavement! But what does the human brain intuitively and naturally do when confronted with a painful or boring activity? He's looking for loopholes. It is on this observation that Henri Laborit relied to elaborate his theory on the management of time at work: the animal instinct of the man pushes him to privilege the activities which give him pleasure and to postpone those that bother him or cause him trouble. The human is thus done and whether or not he is at his workplace does not change anything: his mind will lead him to seek means of escape. And this is where the specificity of our time gives procrastination a fertile breeding ground. What do you mean?

To understand it, let's take an example. Have you ever seen the Mad Men series? This American series that tells the story of an advertising agency in the 50s and 60s? So, imagine yourself in the 1950s, say, in 1953. You are a woman, a copywriter, and work in an agency on Madison Avenue. But, it's hot ... the weather is long ... you're fed up and want to get out of town and go shopping ... can you do it? No, because you can not leave your office and come back without being spotted. Now, imagine yourself in 2016. You are still a woman, a copywriter, in a Madison Avenue agency. Today too you are fed up and want to escape a bit to go shopping. Can you do it? Yes! All you need is a few clicks on your computer, tablet, or smartphone, and here you are window-shopping!

In addition, if work is often synonymous with stress, browsing the net is, in turn, a source of pleasure and freedom. Professor Piers Steel, in an interview with Inside Higher ED, considers that the Internet, video games, and social networks, are now the vectors of procrastination. The Sud-Ouest newspaper of May 13, 2016, publishes, for its part, the figures of Olfeo. According to this software publisher, the French, at their place of work, spend more than 2 hours a day surfing the Internet for personal reasons. The majority oxygenates the brain by browsing on Youtube, Facebook, and Wikipedia.

If procrastination makes it possible to flee momentarily an uncomfortable situation, it nonetheless remains itself a source of stress. In fact, procrastinators often experience dissatisfaction, apprehension of tomorrow (inevitably!), And a lack of esteem. Can we remedy this phenomenon?

Procrastination at work: solutions exist

"We procrastinate, you procrastinate, they procrastinate." What was the interest of this exercise for little Herve? Make him aware that he tends to procrastinate. We can not correct a problem until we become aware of its existence. Then, understand this: to put a problem overnight is useless because it will always be present. In addition, tomorrow always arrives faster than you think. Instinctively, the postponement thinks he will be better e□uipped to do this job, but that is a mistake. So, what to do?

Kaizen ...

What is it about? Many methods exist to fight against procrastination. Today, we present you with one that is making its way into corporate management, both in Japan and in the West. The Kaizen method has been imagined as a rule of life applicable to work and personal life. It consists of performing for 1 minute each day and at the same time, a task that we do not like, until it does not cause us any more stress. But, more generally, it is a matter of rectifying a gap gradually, not brutally. As far as procrastination is concerned, the strategy consists, not in suppressing it, but in gradually reducing it, until it is freed from it. For example, how much time do you spend each day procrastinating?. About ... 1 hour? .. 2 hours? .. If it's 1 hour, decide that, from tomorrow, you will procrastinate, but for 55 minutes. Decide that the day after tomorrow you will procrastinate, but for 50 minutes. Decide that next week you will procrastinate, but for 30 minutes. Decide that you will put an end to your procrastination, but calmly, gently, without hurting yourself. The Kaizen method is a continual and small improvement. Are you ready for the challenge? it is continuous improvement and small touches. Are you ready for the challenge? it is continuous improvement and small touches. Are you ready for the challenge?

Solutions To Avoid Procrastination And Increase Its Productivity

Take an interest in existing time management methods

Many people who are new to their personal development are interested in the different methods of time management known to better plan their actions. This good reflex is excellent advice to fight naturally procrastination.

Being able to organize his time, we fight the urge to postpone the task that bothers us. This simply because one is aware that it must be done since you have integrated it into a system. In this case, delaying the deadline could upset your entire schedule.

Learn to focus on the real priorities

Becoming aware of the importance of carrying out your actions is a sure way of determining which tasks to perform first. Understand and identify the urgency so that you never forget important things that can not be reported anymore.

Set consistent and achievable goals

One of the fundamental principles of personal effectiveness is knowing how to define one's goals clearly. Even if it sounds simple said like that, there are many people who never take the time to make such a report. Yet setting goals can be a big step for your personal accomplishment.

By simply writing down the projects that are most important to you, you will see more clearly in your life. Be careful, however, to make sure you do not set unrealistic goals, at the risk of depressing you unnecessarily.

Stay focused and no longer be distracted

Difficult not to postpone when we are systematically interrupted in our work. Whether it's the vibrating phone, the flashing Facebook notification, or the long-time friend who comes to visit you ... There will always be a good excuse to delay the deadline. And so rejected at the last moment this task that you avoid with fervor.

Except that in the end, the result of the races is that you have to do everything urgently. In addition to putting you in a state of panic never pleasant to live, it reinforces your guilt.

To avoid these inconveniences, it is better to do everything possible to stay focused on your work and no longer let any trivial distraction disturb your personal organization.

To regain self-confidence and one's abilities

Procrastinating often leads to a deep sense of guilt. The constant postponement of tasks haunts you, and you feel blame for dealing with the situation in a hurry when you have plenty of time to do the job before.

If you're wondering how to handle this, it's just going to have to start believing in you again.

If you assume that you will not succeed, no miracle will happen. Trust yourself, you say you can.

Putting yourself in this positive state of mind is the only way to end the discouragement and devaluation of self-esteem.

Get rid of the fastest tasks to perform

Often, looking at one's to-do list, one is already discouraged in advance. So much to do, and so little time to do it all! The time is not yet extensible, and even if it's a shame, you may be mistaken.

So dry your tears and take this list together, do you want. I have the solution to all your troubles.

Cut out his work to stay motivated

Once you've cleaned up your impressive list of goals by immediately completing tasks that take less than two minutes, you'll end up logically with the things to do the most time-consuming. Faced with this kind of "projects", we can ☐uickly let go and fall back into the trap of procrastination again.

The solution to deal with this feeling of discouragement is to simply cut larger tasks into faster sub-actions. Thus, the objectives to be achieved are less impressive and they will appear to you more easily achievable.

Sometimes, simply prioritizing a project can easily increase your productivity.

Fight the urge to postpone

If one of the deadly sins that dominate you the most is laziness, then the urge to procrastinate may sometimes come back to tickle you. Resist the enemy. Personal organization is not just a matter of management.

Motivation plays a vital role in your success.

If you're wondering how to stop procrastinating, the most logical answer to give you is to simply regain self-control.

Stop finding excuses because there is nothing less profitable in the long run.

Build your own organizational method

You will need to experiment with some methodical approaches to be able to build a bespoke system to increase your productivity.

Each person is different and you are no exception to the rule. What works for me will not work for you and vice versa.

It is for this reason that you must remain curious and open to all information available on this subject. The possibilities of organizing yourself correctly are unlimited.

All you have to do is pick up here and there all the tips that will help you better manage your workload.

Do not overwhelm yourself

It is easy to overwhelm a lot of work, meetings and deadlines of all kinds. When tasks seem insurmountable, here is a way to reduce this burden: prepare a "to-do" list, then break it down and follow it. Separating a big task into several elements makes it more manageable. You have your ultimate goal, but by reducing it to smaller components, you have a clearer view of what you need to do.

Performing each small part of an important task that you have to do will give you a sense of accomplishment that you would not have if you tackled the task in one go.

Rewrite the story

I do not care who you are: an employee, a manager or a CEO, you are like everyone else, and we all hate to do certain tasks. So why not change the scenario?

Put this thankless task that you have to do at the top of your day to-do list. This will allow you to move □uickly to the rest of your day. Not to mention that you will have a greater sense of accomplishment knowing that you have overcome the biggest obstacle that awaits you this day.

Forget perfection

Everyone wants to make a good impression at work. Procrastination does not come from the inability to do the job, but from fear and insecurity. Being uncertain about how to perform a specific task scares us, fearing failure, and being viewed with a bad eye by the boss.

If you are concerned about the quality of your work, allocate a fixed amount of time each day to complete (or review) parts of each project. It is possible to perfect a task without spending too much time. That's when you know it's time to let go of the project and focus on other things. Say it with me: no one will die.

Eliminate distractions

It's easy to procrastinate with the million distractions we have every day. In a survey by Stop Procrastinating, 68% of Americans surveyed said they had been distracted from their work by checking email, surfing the web, or surfing social media. This is an increase of 9% over the previous year.

Of course, it is tempting to constantly check your Facebook or Twitter feeds, but here is a radical concept: log out of your social accounts for a few hours, every day.

Instead, focus on your tasks and nothing else. Do whatever it takes to get into your "bubble" to reach your goal. Some people in my office use a headset to stifle outside noise. For my part, I block a niche on my calendar (to which my employees have access) and I dedicate this time to a specific task that I must perform. I can even say "no phone call" to make sure I stay in my bubble.

Method to increase productivity

Increase productivity. Avoid these bad habits

Habit 1. Continue working during vacation We are increasingly inclined to continue working during our vacation. Examples of this are reading and answering work-related messages and phone calls. This keeps us stuck in the work rhythm and we take insufficient rest. But let this holiday just be meant to recharge ourselves - and come back with a fresh look. These habits are slowly but surely becoming a kind of the social norm. It is almost self-evident that employees also go to work during their vacation. And that is not a positive development.

Habit 2.Multitasking Do you know the statement 'Women can multitask and men cannot'? Nothing at all correct! Both men and women cannot multitask. For activities in which we are well trained and can put our mind on automatic pilot (such as listening to music and cycling), switching between brain areas is still quite smooth. This goes so fast that we don't even realize it. It goes wrong when we perform tasks in which we are less well trained. Such as: asking someone during an intensive walk to solve a complicated calculation. The brain must look for the answer, making walking more difficult. Some people even stop moving!

Habit 3. Not including all vacation hours

Scientific research shows that it is important that we actually record all of our vacation hours. Not taking vacation hours has a negative impact on our mood. It also comes at the expense of our social relationships and productivity. So make sure you always record your vacation hours.

Habit 4. Continuing to work during evening hours and during the weekend

We all do this unconsciously. But it is precisely the evening hours and weekends that are meant to rest and clear our heads. Mental breaks ensure that you can go back to work with a fresh perspective. But how can you work with a fresh perspective if you avoid mental breaks? We all know how important and necessary it is to work with a fresh perspective.

Habit 5. Organizing meetings without a clear goal

Are you also tired of meetings that jump from the heel to the branch? This is often because no agenda items and goals have been set in advance. Sometimes agenda items and goals have been set - but not all participants are aware of it. This means you lose a lot of time and you don't get the desired result from meetings.

Habit 6. Failure to complete tasks and chores

Failure to complete tasks and chores causes stress. The attention units go to the unfinished jobs and tasks. As a result, fewer units of attention remain to perform the current work. Increasing your productivity is possible when you finish tasks and chores as much as possible immediately.

Habit 7. Things that didn't work out

Things that didn't work out cause fatigue. If this happens often, or if it is something very big that no longer works, then it can even lead to burnout. Burnout is caused by things that are no longer possible and failed goals. This drastically lowers productivity.

Habit 8.Human emotions and reactions

Human emotions and reactions are the greatest enemies of our productivity. Because people become angry, sad, scared, etc. due to circumstances or because of their environment, they start producing less. Their thought goes entirely to those concerning circumstances that have caused the emotion. This too is at the expense of concentration and drastically reduces productivity.

8 ways to increase your productivity

Do you start the day with all good intentions, but don't get enough done? Then take note of these 8 productivity tips.

1.Save time when reading texts

Long texts are often faster to read than you think. You can often skip paragraphs by two thirds. By reading the first lines of a paragraph, in particular, you can pass passages much faster and still understand the essence. Is there a graph in the piece? If you understand without textual explanation, it will save you a few minutes.

With opinion texts and research reports, you come a long way when you read the first paragraph and the last two paragraphs. It contains the main ⬜uestion, reason, and conclusions. Whoever wants to read paragraphs in full can save time by taking the second or third word for each line as a starting point and ending with the second or third word on the right.

2.Organize at least one meetingless day

Meetings are difficult to ban from the agenda, especially if you are a (top) manager. The problem with meetings is that they often end up. Once a meeting ends, you are out of the rhythm that it is required to function effectively behind your desk. The only way to prevent that is to schedule meetings in one day. This immediately gives you a good excuse for not ending a meeting, otherwise, you miss the next one. The end result is that you have days left on which you can fully focus on the office work.

3.Avoid distractions

Various international studies show that distraction is the first ' cause of death ' of your productivity. Every day you walk into your office with good intentions, and then halfway through the day, you conclude that you have been busy with all sorts of aimless and useless things. Not only does it regularly mean that you visit too many sites that have nothing to do with your work, but you are also chatting too much with colleagues.

Do this only at set times during the day, such as in the morning when everyone walks in, or during lunch. Put a thermos with coffee on your desk on a busy day, so you don't have to walk back and forth to the kitchen.

4.Look for situations in which you work alone

Great, those modern offices in which a workplace is no longer separated, but you are more likely to be distracted by the buzz and phone calls from colleagues. One way to avoid the crowds is to work in the early morning or late evening. You can also look for a quiet place within the office building: walk around the floors, you will often find a separate workspace. The dining room also has lounge areas where you can work undisturbed with your laptop.

5.Stop multitasking

Today we live in a world with multiple screens, which have made us all into multitasking addicts. A recent study by Google shows that 66% of people use smartphones and computers at the same time, while ninety percent of respondents spend all day doing nothing but operating electronic devices. So don't let yourself be distracted unnecessarily by Whatsapp messages. And also stop checking Twitter.

6.Don't let your day be led by email

Because email flows in all day long, you can develop obsessive behavior in which you cannot resist checking your message flow over and over again. But are you really getting along with that? Unless you are waiting for a very important e-mail, it is better to set fixed time periods in which you enter your mailbox. In those hours you fully focus on sending and answering email. Much more effective.

7.Follow the 80/20 rule

It is sometimes said that only 20% of what you do every day produces 80% of your results. That 20% is most fruitful in the period that you still do your work 100% energetically and with focus. If you take that saying as a given, it is smart to plan your most essential tasks at the start of the day. Then at the end of the day, it is easier to accept that you have not been able to complete a number of tasks on your to-do list.

8.Wake up with more energy

Many people do not feel tired in the morning because they would not have slept enough, but because their blood sugar levels are too low. To remedy that, you can adjust your eating habits a little in the evening, without having to stay wide awake. Take for example one or two tablespoons of unsweetened almond butter.

Take the time you need to start over

Thinking that you have the future in your own hands is a two-sided sword: on the one hand, this thought offers certainty and vitality, but on the other, it can create a huge gap. Starting again means, among other things, that you have to finish certain things and let go. Something about it didn't go well and it could even have been painful.

Starting over again means becoming aware of something that needs to change in your life, becoming aware that you need to heal your wounds so that you can look to the future in a new way.

Timing is, as we said, essential in situations where we feel lost. This is the only way we can reform our principles. From the moment we realize that we have to start over, we will notice that something has changed in us and that we are no longer the same person as before: we have to get to know ourselves again.

In order to build new relationships with other people, to further develop ourselves in a certain area of our lives or just to be happy with what we are doing, it is necessary to once again experience emotional blockages get a good idea of who we really are.

Not giving yourself enough time for this is one of the most common mistakes we make as human beings. We are already ready to start again when the damage may not have been fully repaired.

Not giving yourself enough time can lead to regression

Preparing yourself usually re☐uires time. And the time it requires is actually relative: there is no fixed calculation for this. The only rule that could be attached to it is that we must look at, among other things, the degree of inner loss, pain, willpower, and strength. Everyone is different and our ability to deal with difficult situations is also different.

What is certain is that, as with every process, there are a few guidelines associated with starting over. And if you do not follow these guidelines, you may suffer from regression. Sometimes we think we are prepared to face a new beginning until suddenly the reality pops up and completely engulfs us. This is how it is made clear to us that we have made a mistake and that we still have a lot to do.

A major effort will be rewarded

This process has its ups and downs and requires one of the greatest efforts we will ever have to make in life. Not looking back is difficult, accepting something that we do not understand is difficult, learning to live without something we could count on before is heartbreaking and seeing someone leave our lives way too early is overwhelming.

However, we can also learn a lot from other things that we did not know before and that can help us to grow. The effort we have to make to endure such situations will eventually turn the experience into a positive reward that can fill us with experience and happiness.

Ultimately, through a lot of sacrifices, we will feel emotionally free and complete again. We will be able to understand what we have been through and have learned to be content with what we have in the present. We will be able to live our lives according to the new principles that we have reformed. It will be a new start after a phase in your life that has come to an end.

11 tips to find focus and improve productivity

1.GET YOUR MINDSET RIGHT

Everything, but then everything starts with your mindset. When your mindset is not right, being maximally productive and being focused is impossible.

How are you currently doing in every area of life?

Are you satisfied with how things are going?

Are you uncertain and worried about certain matters?

How did you get up this morning? What were the first thoughts that came to mind?

We are often not aware of the many internal dialogues. The danger of this is that you want to start your day in a focused way, but that thoughts are constantly going through your head:

"Aiii, last night I noticed that my partner was not well. What will be the matter with him/her? "

"Hmm, a customer has an overdue payment, when will he pay?"

"I have to do so much today, but I have no overview at all. Where do I begin?"

So many different internal dialogues can take place that it is important to tackle them first. If you do not feel optimally (uncertainty, sadness and other negative emotions), first resolve these emotions otherwise they will hinder you in maintaining focus. You lose focus most quickly because of the negative thoughts and emotions that go through your head.

Advice: Become aware of your negative emotions and resolve them immediately.

2.DETERMINE YOUR FOCUS GOAL AND MAKE IT SPECIFIC

What is your most important goal? And I'm talking about your really most important goal. What do you want to achieve this year, this month and this week? What is really the most important goal that sets you in motion as an entrepreneur.

Too many entrepreneurs are constantly busy with simple tasks that hardly contribute to the growth of their business. Investigate what really matters to you? Determine a large but achievable goal and work towards it in steps. Those steps, or milestones, make your goal specific.

This way, your larger goal for this year can be: € 200,000 in revenue. Only this is not specific yet. By establishing milestones you make it clear.

Milestones:

Generate 600 leads per month

Based on the 600 leads I want 4 conversations per week

At least 1 new customer per week comes out of the 4 conversations per week

New customers per month at € 5,000 per new customer = € 20,000 per month

Q1: 12 new customers for € 60,000 in total

1 year: 40 new customers for € 200,000 in total

By setting milestones you also immediately know what your focus should be. You also know what is important to you and therefore what is not. If you get a call today to speak for free somewhere, then you first have to ask yourself if this fits your purpose and therefore your focus.

Advice: Set your goals for this year and divide them into quarters, months and weeks. Do everything that brings you closer to your goal and ignore/turn off the things that do not bring you closer to your goal.

3.MAKE A FOCUS PRIORITY LIST

When you have determined your focus goal, it is now time to establish a priority list. After all, your milestones do not yet substantively reflect what needs to be done. In the example for tip 2 you know that you want to generate 600 leads per month, but you do not yet know how.

Therefore make a list (marketing strategy) how you will get there. What is the first step, the next and the next? First make a list and stop everything on paper. You will then classify these tasks based on priorities. Then continue to tip 4.

4.PLAN YOUR MONTH, WEEK AND DAY

Now that you know what your goals and priorities are, you plan to plan them consistently every month, week and day. One of the pitfalls of entrepreneurs is that they have no planning or that they do, but that they do not stick to it. I know, because I didn't have a schedule regularly, so I started a week without knowing what was really important. I also saw it with many former customers (in the area of marketing strategy). They did not meet their deadlines because the focus was missing.

Buy an offline calendar. Then you do not have the distraction that the online version entails. Of course you can also use an online agenda (after all, I do that too), but then do it in the following way:

Put all your tasks that come to mind (such as appointments, etc.) in your online agenda (or note down other forms of tasks).

Take over the tasks in your offline agenda every Sunday and plan them in blocks of 50 minutes (see tip 8).

Advice: As you can see above, I advise you to prepare your schedule for a Sunday paper agenda. That way you can get started immediately on Monday. This brings me directly to point number 5 ...

5.FOCUS YOURSELF & SHUTDOWN DISTRACTION

Social media, e-mail, news and so on: shut it down! All these activities take away the focus and certainly do not make you more productive as an entrepreneur. Research shows that you are 20% less productive when you start checking your day with social media or the mailbox.

Why? Because at that moment you deal with the needs and agendas of other people. You will not find things in your mailbox or on social media that contribute to your focus. It is meaningless and unnecessary.

You grab your focus by starting your day with your one-thing. The most important task that brings your company forward. Entrepreneurs who make breakthrough after breakthrough are aware of their one-thing. These are the entrepreneurs who get up at least 1 hour earlier than they are used to and spend that extra hour on their one thing.

6.DETERMINE YOUR INTENTIONS

Do you determine your intentions on a daily basis or is this area still unknown to you? Determining intentions gives a boost to both your focus and your productivity. Every time I start a new activity, I close my eyes and imagine how I want to behave during this activity. What are my intentions?

I want to be focused on this task.

I give 100% love and attention to the client I coach.

Even though something is not my favorite task, I want to experience pleasure and be in the moment.

Advice: Determine your intentions every time you start a new activity

7.DISCIPLINE YOURSELF TO FOCUS

Are you a discipline person or a motivation person ? If you ask me, motivation is weak and discipline is what you need to be focused and boost your productivity. Therefore, also work on your discipline.

If you have planned to work out at 9:00 AM, do so and do not get distracted by a phone call coming in from a customer you need. Chances are that if you pick up the phone certain things are re□uired of you and that you will sacrifice your sport for that.

The same applies to working on a task. Have the discipline to keep focusing and do not be seduced by your cell phone or tabs that are open on your computer and that are crying out for attention.

Advice: Close unnecessary tabs, switch off your mobile phone and tell any colleagues that you do not want to be disturbed.

8.WORK IN BLOCKS OF 50 MINUTES

Many studies show that you can only be optimally busy for 50 minutes. Nice to do these investigations, but we all know from practice. You have certainly worked on a task for more than 50 minutes and at some point a sort of brain overload occurred .

Your head is full at such a moment, but you still want to push the task through.

Not effective and certainly not useful for your focus. You tackle this problem by working in blocks of 50 minutes, followed by 10 breathing exercises, stretching exercises, going to the toilet, drinking 2 glasses of water and popping again. When you do that, you give your brain time to reset itself so that they can continue fresh afterwards.

We often think that we are very productive. After discovering the 5 × 50 productivity formula, entrepreneurs soon realize that they are often not very productive at all.

9.RELEASE YOUR FOCUS DAILY (MEDITATION, YOGA, SPORTS)

Release! Now? Yes, why not! Close your eyes for a moment, focus on your breathing and take a 10x deep breath.

How does it feel? Pretty good or not? Or did you not do it? (sigh ...) ;-)

Letting go is extremely important if you want to be focused and productive. Your brain only has a certain capacity and you don't want a brain overload. Therefore plan daily moments of relaxation and rest.

That is not :

check social media

netflixing or watching TV

read news etc.

But correct:

hiking

meditation

yoga

10.FOCUS BY SAYING "NO"

"Say no!" "No!" Okay ... I just got a Tony Robbins moment. How often do you say "no" during the day? Not often? Do you now understand why you often lose your focus and your productivity is not optimal?

People often get distracted. Whether it's by colleagues, their cell phone or a sudden event. Our brains are constantly active to get us out of our focus and flow.

Therefore, dare to say "NO".

No, I don't have time for you right now because I'm working on this and I want to finish it at 10:00 a.m.

No, I don't pick up the phone, because this activity is now leading. At 2 p.m. I have a fixed time to call.

No, I am not checking my mailbox now, because that does not make me productive.

No no no no!

Decide for yourself:

Are you in charge of your agenda?

Are other people reading (social media, telephone, mailbox) in charge of your agenda?

When you want to be the boss (take leadership) you say "No" to everything, because you have already completed your planning for the day.

Advice: Always say no, but clearly state that you want to help and indicate when you will do so. You do that at a fixed time that you block. That is leadership.

11.DRINK, EAT AND SLEEP ENOUGH

DRINK

Your brain consists of 73% water. If you drink too little water, then your brain cannot function normally. What I always do myself is, after getting up, drink 2 glasses of water and during the rest of the day about 5 liters of water. Sounds a lot, it is, but focus and productivity are important things to me.

Yes, you have to go to the toilet more often and that's good because then you move immediately too. So check if you drink enough water during the day. If you do not do this, then chances are that you often lose your focus quickly because your brain cannot perform optimally.

FOOD

Good food is also very important. I myself eat in a modified paleo way. During the week I don't eat meat (only on special occasions) and focus on eating a shit-load of vegetables. This choice ensures that I am in a high energy and therefore very productive and can keep my focus well. In addition, it is also true that I only eat twice a day, at 12 p.m. and 5 p.m. and that my body needs no food for the rest of the day.

Eating has a big influence on your productivity and focus, especially if you are constantly high in carbohydrates, etc. because your body is constantly peaking and you then fall back in sugars. That is not great for your focus. So consider for yourself what the influence of food is on your focus and productivity.

TO SLEEP

Do you drink enough and do you eat healthily? In addition, ensure at least 7 hours of sleep per night. It has been proven that after an extended period of time, sleeping less than 7 hours a night functions cognitively the same as after drinking 4 glasses of alcohol.

Seven hours of sleep means that you will take it easy 1 hour before sleeping. Avoid the TV and other blue screens (such as your mobile). Prepare yourself as a bear enters his cave. You will not see a bear running, no, he goes slow, very slow.

When you are in bed, make sure that you can stay in bed for at least another 7 hours and 30 minutes. After all, you need time to get into a deep sleep. I use magnesium every night before going to sleep. My sleep is very deep (I dream a lot every night) and I feel well rested in the morning and wake up by my biological clock instead of by an alarm clock.

Advice: drink 2 large glasses of water at least every 50 minutes, avoid junk food and other bad food.

How to overcome distraction and get into the ultimate learning flow

Tip 1:Determine a goal

We can never learn something effectively if we don't know why we learn it at all. A chapter about space figures (mathematics) sounds like a heavy birth to many, at least to me. "Why the hell am I supposed to learn this?" You might think. In itself, it has no connection with your personal goals and it just motivates you. So something is needed that links the chapter to yourself. Questions you can ask yourself are: What do I want to be? What do I want to achieve? What are my benefits if I have learned this chapter? What does it contribute to my goal? Visualize the answers so that you get the motivation and energy to get through.

Tip 2:Keep remembering the value of your goal

As humans, we will always give priority to the activity that gives us the most benefit. If a classmate interrupts you while learning to ask for a favor, you will probably see his / her approval and appreciation as more valuable than completing your learning task. So we distract ourselves because we see the new task as more valuable than the task we were doing. So it's important to keep remembering the value of your goal.

Tip 3: Set long-term satisfaction above short-term satisfaction

Searching for short-term satisfaction is something we do all the time. The only way to overcome this is to nurture your motivation. Reward yourself for your perseverance. For example, after each chapter learned, you do something or give yourself something that you think is super cool. Write down the rewards so that you can stay focused on the longer term.

Tip 4: Prevent boredom

If we learn or do something that is not that interesting for us, a distraction such as viewing our social media can give us more energy and satisfaction. So we choose that. If this is the case, make the task more interesting for yourself. How can you make the process more interesting towards your goal? Is your goal interesting enough? Find a way to make the process mentally and emotionally stimulating for yourself.

Tip 5: Eliminate fear

Thoughts of fear can get in the way of your performance. Of course it's important to start on time, I don't have to tell you that. But the essence of this thought lies mainly in the feeling of pressure. ¨ I am only good enough if I succeed. I have to do this! ¨ is a wrong motivator and causes a lot of unnecessary stress. A better and more relaxed motivation is "I am good enough already, I don't have to prove anything but I want to do this." That way you take the pressure off the boiler and make your mind clear again, which is needed to get into the flow.

6 tips for the ultimate focus

If at the end of the day you think back to the tasks you have all completed, do you remember what you did exactly? Do you know that feeling that you have been busy all day with phone calls and e-mails, but you are not one step further with the things you really had to do? Working deeply concentrated without being distracted: how do you do that?

1.Set priorities

Performing one or two tasks on your workday, where your priority is, is a lot more effective than doing half a job. Make a schedule to make it easier for yourself to focus. If you focus on one specific task at a time, instead of multitasking, you will achieve a much better result.

2.Work in blocks of time

Spending hours behind a computer can sometimes lead to amazing results. Yet after 1.5 hours, most people have a hard time staring at that screen.

Headache, dry eyes and energy-free work is no fun for anyone.

Working in blocks of time prevents this and gives you a moment to give your head a rest. Intensive work requires intensive breaks. Just do nothing for 10 minutes and get back to work. Alternating between a time block with deeply concentrated work and a lighter task is according to Cal Newport a way to strengthen your concentration.

3.Close

Whatsapp, e-mail, talking colleagues around you, phone calls, appointments; we let ourselves be distracted throughout the day by things that happen around us. Therefore choose a workplace with little distraction / noise, but that is not so ☐uiet that you are dazed. Discover which place keeps you sharp and get to work! Also indicate to your colleagues that you are temporarily unavailable and approachable. Can you close the door? To do!

For many people it is a bad habit to be constantly available.

This ensures that you can never have 100% focus on anything else. Do you really want to work deeply concentrated? Then switch off all your devices (okay, at least on silent) and put them away. Do you still have to work on a computer? Turn off your mail and stay away from social media and news sites.

4.Use a worry block

Are you really ready, but are you distracted by your thoughts? Leiden University gives as a concentration tip the use of a 'worry block'. Write down briefly what you are doing, put a line under it and continue with your work. You park your thoughts, as it were, to take your time at a later time.

5.Drink plenty of water

Are you familiar with the afternoon dip around 3 or 4 in the afternoon? This dip is mainly due to dehydration; 80% of your brain consists of water, says life success coach Sven Veenstra . Drinking enough water ensures a stable energy level and therefore a stable concentration. This makes you more productive.

During your dip, skip the coffee and go for a glass of water.

6.Relax as soon as possible!

Take a moment to relax every day. Do something that you like and makes you feel good. Newport believes in emptiness and tran☐uility. His tip: be lazy. With deeply concentrated work, a healthy dose of free time is re☐uired. Relaxing also means that you do not read work emails in the evenings and during the weekend.

The more aware you are of what you want and what is happening around you that prevents you from achieving your goal, the more proactive you can be in changing it. With these tips you have to come to an end when it comes to concentrated work. Is concentration not a problem for you, but does your productivity not increase? Perhaps you are guilty of these 4 bad habits that make you extremely unproductive.

Set priorities or learn to prioritize

The definition of prioritizing is: prioritizing. Those who find it difficult to set priorities must and want to do everything at the same time. The result: it is too much, too big and nothing ends up. We set priorities every day and often unconsciously. When you walk to the car, you may sooner forget your sunglasses than your car keys. This also applies to your time management. When you start the day with writing a quote you give priority to this task. But is this also an important task at that time or does your customer expect the □uotation only after four weeks?

So prioritizing is: 'doing the right things at the right time'. But what is correct? You are the only one who can assess this, possibly together with the re□uirements that the organization sets for you.

Action list: urgent and important

Prioritizing starts with creating an action list on which you list all tasks. We distinguish between important and urgent. It is sometimes difficult to identify that difference, but we will apply it to your situation as much as possible

Important: It must be completed, if you don't do it, problems will arise. Important tasks often belong to the core of your position.

Unimportant: It will not have serious conse uences if you do not take this action.

Urgent: It must happen today or this week.

Not urgent: It doesn't matter when you perform the task

Make choices

Setting priorities means making choices. First, you must determine: what is important and what is urgent, what is not important and what is not urgent.

Urgent and important

Tasks of priority 1 are urgent and important: so do it immediately. These tasks always have priority. Examples: urgent matters, issues or problems, crisis situations and all activities that are subject to a deadline.

Important but not urgent

Priority 2 tasks are important but not urgent. So you still have time. Plan it and start on time. You can think of preparations for the following year or for meetings, policy development, vision and strategy development, relationship management and maintenance, planning for the coming months.

Urgent but not important

Priority 3 tasks are urgent but not important. The urgency can make it happen today, otherwise, you don't have to do it anymore. You can think of meetings that matter less, phone calls that you are not waiting for, some e-mails or mail items that do not. Example: you have been approached for market research and you want to participate. It's not that important to you, but you have one day left to respond. You will be late tomorrow.

Not important and not urgent

Priority 9 tasks are neither important nor urgent. This can be the umpteenth representative who calls you for an appointment while you have no interest in it. But also other trivial matters, some telephone conversations or useless meetings. So don't, unless you have a lot of time left.

Setting priorities prevents stress. 6 valuable tips!

Setting priorities helps if you don't know what to do first and what can wait until later. A pity, because time is precious and you want to spend it as well as possible. This applies both at home and at work. Read valuable tips below to gain control of your life. Your profit? More overview, peace of mind and less tension.

1.Empty your head with an overview

Making an overview - to-do list - of what you have to do, sounds cliché. But setting priorities without a task list is very difficult. It helps to clear your head and get an overview. Both with regard to your work and your private life. Take a sheet of paper and pen and write it off. Which activities, tasks, jobs, plans, etc. you must and want to do. Are you ready? Then arrange everything in order of urgency. What must be done today? What can wait until tomorrow, next week or even next month? By making such a to-do list, you can set priorities much better, you clear your head and you experience less stress.

2.Allow yourself sufficient time and stop multitasking

Then make sure you allow sufficient time for each task. That way you have plenty of time to do your thing calmly. After all, sometimes it may take a little longer to complete something than you think. Also, do not do other small activities during your job, such as calling or checking your e-mail. Not only does your attention relax, but you also disrupt your workflow, which means you spend more time than planned. So take your time and do not multitask, because then you run the risk of not getting the to do's off your list, which will make you tense.

3.Set limits and say 'no'

Setting priorities also means knowing your limits. So clearly state what you can do so that someone else knows. And do not say 'yes' everywhere if you are called upon. No matter how nice you seem. You also want to save time for your hobbies, sports, children, partner, friends and so on. So, be clear and set limits and feel free to say 'no'.

4.Asking for help is also setting priorities

Asking others for help is not a weakness at all. Because say for yourself: doing everything in your own house is sometimes ☐uite difficult. Even if you think you are an expert in certain matters. Many hands make light work. So don't hesitate and delegate or outsource tasks. To your colleague, domestic help, babysitter or partner. You get more space so that you can better focus on what you find important. Moreover, you can avoid disappointment because otherwise, you will not finish your work.

5.Also, do what gives you energy

Do you keep buffering without doing what gives you energy? Then there is a good chance that stress builds up slowly in you. You become restless, feel tired and irritable. Is suffering from sleeplessness, is restless and has tense neck and shoulder muscles. In fact, the puff is sort of out. Do you recognize that? Then prioritizing is becoming increasingly difficult. Prevent that and regularly incorporate relaxation moments in your life. Take a wonderful walk, visit the sauna, listen to your favorite music, go dancing, play sports, play football with your children, meditate, spend the weekend and go out for dinner with your partner. Charging your battery regularly helps relax, provides energy and fights stress.

6.Take care of yourself and live healthily

A healthy mind lives in a healthy body. Therefore, take good care of yourself. Eat good and healthy foods, drink 2 to 2.5 liters of fluid a day, exercise regularly, maintain your social contacts. Now and then laze a day and get enough sleep. In this way you are positive in your life, you feel fit, you feel the energy and priorities and compliance are a lot easier.

How to get things done and stop procrastination

Don't get overwhelmed by the task

If you become overweight due to a task, the resulting fear can inadvertently make you inactive. To prevent that, everything revolves around the way you think. Train yourself to believe that you can get things done even if it doesn't feel right.

Learn to recognize negative thinking patterns and get rid of them. Use the catastrophe scale to gain perspective when a task seems too difficult to complete.

Change your attitude to the task

Have you ever heard someone say that you need a posture change? If so, you are not the only one. Have a surly or otherwise negative view This depression and anxiety test will help you understand your emotions This depression and anxiety test will help you understand your emotions There are too many people who deny about depression, anxiety, and stress. Use this self-assessment test to see where you are with each of the three and what you can do about it. Read more about responsibility can be debilitating. Ultimately you can convince yourself that a task is not worth trying and deciding that you would rather face the consequences.

The tips for setting goals help you create goals that you can really achieve. Achieving goals must lead to a more positive attitude. You can also follow progress over time. When you find yourself steadily heading in the right direction, your mood should get a boost. In addition, metrics allow you to make smarter decisions if things don't go well, thereby preventing discouragement.

Work with your biorhythm

If you normally wake up at the same time without an alarm, you respond to circadian rhythms. They mainly respond to light and darkness, but also affect issues such as lung capacity and hormone production. Some people also claim that alignment with circadian rhythms can maximize productivity. Can that get you out of procrastination?

Postpone positively

Postponing can be positive if you feel good about it. If your energy behind is positive. If you have a 'good' reason for delaying. For example, an inspiring appointment, which on the contrary motivates you to get down to work. Or an afternoon with your girlfriend that you haven't seen for too long.

Then you consciously choose something else. Something nice, something that makes you happy. And that is allowed! Then you choose to do 'what should be done' at a different time.

SUCCESSFUL PEOPLE AVOID PROCRASTINATION IN THESE 5 WAYS

1.THEY FEEL RESPONSIBLE

Make an appointment with yourself to get things done. That way you feel responsible. Write down your goals, for example, keep a to-do list on paper or on your phone. Successful people remind themselves of tasks in different ways. For example, put a post-it on your computer screen, make a list and put important tasks on the agenda of your mailbox. Every time you see your tasks, you feel responsible for them. Moreover, tell them to colleagues, bosses or friends. That way you feel extra responsible and they will talk to you about it if you lose sight of them.

2.THEY STAY AWAY FROM SOCIAL MEDIA

It is tempting to ☐uickly check your Whatsapp during work hours, look on Facebook or read the latest news. But successful people focus on just one task, the task they have to perform. For the same reason, they also view their emails only a few times a day, at set times. By closing your mailbox you will not be distracted every time an email arrives.

3.PLAN THEM

Everything stands or falls with good planning. How often do you start your workday, start looking at what you have to work on and are you actually reading your emails? If you start your day without an idea that you should actually start with, it is much easier to postpone. Therefore, try to complete all your to-do list for the next day the day before. Think about what you did on the day and what you still have to do. In addition, view what has the highest priority.

4.THEY BREAK UP A LARGE TASK INTO SEVERAL SMALL TASKS

Large tasks can ☐uickly feel overwhelming. Successful people know that all too well. That's why they split their tasks into smaller ones. Make sure the points on your list are measurable and realistic. For example, an author would not have the goal of "write book," but "write at least 1000 words today."

5.THEY ARE SELF-AWARE

Most successful people are aware of their own strengths and weaknesses. If you know why you postpone, it is also easier to tackle your procrastination. Take a step back and ask yourself why you are delaying. Boredom, lack of confidence or feeling overwhelmed are just some of the possible reasons. By being aware of that you can tackle the cause.

Monitor emotions . Deliberately ask yourself what you feel in the event of interruptions. Most interruptions are learned strategies to avoid unpleasant emotions. If you are more aware of the reasons for interrupting your work, you can use more effective strategies to deal with this.

Choose fast success . By this, the author means that you have to deal with simple tasks that cause a lot of unrest. A 'to do' list always attracts attention. Relatively simple tasks often require a disproportionate amount of attention. Be the first to complete tasks that only take a few minutes.

Organize loneliness . Reserve time and space for focus. Choose the moments when you are most productive, and then block time and (physical) space to work on complex tasks with concentration. Switch off telephones and notifications, and even avoid access to the internet (in any case, social media). According to Grenny, you need to create a temporary and physical oasis for yourself to work with focus. I regularly use the ' Focus ' application for this . You then indicate how much time you are now going to work on a certain task. The application alerts you when the time is up.

Practice attention . Take, for example, more and more time just to think about an issue. For example, use travel time (public transport) to sit still and put your mind in a row. Switch off all media. Start at five minutes, and gradually expand.

Work on your problems while walking . If your work environment makes it difficult to work without interruption, you can also develop a 'walking plan'. Choose an interesting and important problem and think about it while walking. Moreover, this body activity promotes the functioning of the brain.

TIME MANAGEMENT TIPS

Tip-1.Make sure you have the right motivation

An empty inbox and a well- arranged agenda may be nice and nice, but it is of course not the deeper motivation why you want to better plan your time. There is more to it:

Choosing what you want to manage your time better is not about tightly coordinated task lists. It is a matter of choosing what you want to spend your time on. It is more time left for the things that really matter.

Determining why you want to gain more control over the issues that are now before you is, therefore, the first, and perhaps most important, step. So ask yourself 2 questions:

In what way would I benefit if I gained more control over my time and tasks?

You will make fewer mistakes in your work, finish that project within the deadline and, in addition, be really busy with the right things. Plus points.

What effect does it have on my nearby environment?

As soon as you know what you are doing and why it is easier for you to justify your choices to yourself, but also to the people who want to manage your planning.

As soon as you make clear to yourself what effect a change in your work and lifestyle has on yourself and your environment, your motivation to continue is more stable.

After all, dealing with your time more effectively is not the goal, it is a means to a life in which you have more time for the really important things. That is what you think of on your deathbed, not that empty inbox! So start by creating an overview:

Tip-2.Check regularly where your attention is

There are of course periods that are busier and more stressful than normal. Do you notice that the unrest and stress creep back into your head? Is it still teeming with unfinished tasks? Prevent it by regularly passing through a broom:

For example, take 20 minutes each Friday afternoon to clear your head with a mini thought dump. Think of it as weekly maintenance, so you get your overview up to date again. Plan it in your diary or put it in your phone as a reminder, no matter how you remind yourself: repeat and make a habit of it!

Or do it like genius Bill Gates and take a ' Think-Week '; a week away from civilization to put everything together! (A ' Think-Day' is of course also allowed! Take a day off and check your priorities; have things been added and are the previous ones still relevant?)

So regularly consider issues that re□uire your attention and map them again, so that you have a clearer and clearer picture of what is going on in your own life.

Tip-3.Prioritize your thought dump in 3 steps

Urgent, important? You now understand how the fork works. So apply these time management tips yourself with the thought dump you created earlier. Take that one. Now go task by task, a project by project and look critically at what should be done with it.

1. First, ask yourself 3 □uestions :

What are my important tasks/projects at the moment?

Which actions can only I carry out and belong to the core of my position?

What is now the most valuable use of my time?

2. Then place your task in the 'Eisenhower model' :

Urgent and important? Do it now immediately

Important but not urgent? Plan it in your agenda or put it on your to-do list.

Urgent but not important? See if you can have someone else perform the task.

Not urgent and not important? Delete it from your list.

3. Get started :

This is where the real magic happens. Here you will divide your tasks into a watertight time management system. We will come back to this later!

What is important now is that from now on you will not have to process such a full list of tasks. How? By learning to indicate your limits better;

Tip-4.Say "no" more often from now on and regain control of your life

Do you say " yes " to every project that you are presented with? Own fault, because in this way activities and obligations continue to accumulate. It ensures that you remain chronically busy and in addition, you are concerned with matters that you may not even like. Saying " no " is the only way to regain control of your daily life.

Therefore, take a critical look at your biggest time-consuming obligations. Matters that are important, urgent or can only be performed by you are not taken into account. You do this because they belong to your job description, for example. The rest? Do you not feel any screaming enthusiasm? Say "no" and stop investing your precious time.

How?

Don't you wanna do it?

Do not turn around it. Does your colleague ask if you can 'read' that report? First of all, show that you are not immediately enthusiastic about it. Use a short silence, count yourself to 3 and then say very simply: "No."

Give an alternative. By proposing a different solution, your colleague still feels as if you have been helpful.

"No. I cannot read the report, but I know that the trainee wants to gain insight into the work process. Maybe you can let him do it? "

Do you want to do it, but not now?

Move it. If you want to do it at a later time, you can indicate that:

" No. Not right now, but I can watch it this afternoon. "

Set priorities. Do you want to do it for sure, but will your entire schedule be affected? Just remind your colleague that your schedule is already sufficient and that this will have to shift another task.

"Perhaps. I will, therefore, have to shift my planning with other priorities. What would you like to be the first to do? "

Saying ' no ' is difficult? Not if you do it in this diplomatic way. Regardless of whether it concerns private or business matters, saying 'no' is a magic word that ensures that you are in charge of your own time. Did you, unfortunately, say 'yes' too often in the past and are you burdened with too high a workload? Indicate it:

Tip-5.Make your work pressure negotiable

Is your 'thought-dump list' full of all sorts of things that do not really belong to your position, but which your boss still expects to be done? Did you keep on working after work because otherwise that one project would not be finished? Perhaps you are dealing with a too high workload.

Annoying, sure, but nothing that cannot be solved. The first thought that probably comes to mind is that you especially do not need to raise with your boss. He may think that you cannot handle the tasks or are irresponsible. Nothing is less true;

"Saying no to a high workload is the opposite of failure. Preventing failure. "

So take the initiative, put your boss around the table and indicate it in 3 steps:

1. Emphasize the company vision

You don't have to argue about the vision of the company, but you can indicate that the organization wants to deliver the highest possible quality:

"I know our organization stands for a constant level of quality. I can 100% agree with that ... "

2. Emphasize the pressure problem

It is impossible to deliver perfection day in, day out. Indicate that the workload hinders your functioning:

"... I have recently noticed, however, that the workload is so high and that the pursuit of this quality has fallen into the background. That feels wrong ... "

3. Come up with the solution (s)

Finally, you present a number of solutions with which you could tackle the problem:

"... To solve that problem and reduce my workload, I think it's smart to do [task x] every quarter from now on instead of every month."

You have not only brought up the issue, but you have also shown that you think along with your boss and the organization. Your boss will certainly not care less about you and will even appreciate that you have taken the responsibility to make this point open to discussion.